Awakening Your
Dreams

Seven Principles To
Create A Life You Love

GARY L. WILKIN

ISBN: 978-1-956914-53-5

CONTENTS

To Beth –

*My life partner, my best friend, my wife –
without you, I would not be complete.*

To Francis –

*Thank you for your example
of aging with courage.*

FREE RESOURCE:

Gain clarity and take action as you create a life you love.

Download your free Awakening Your Dreams Action
Journal to record your thoughts, ideas, and plans as you
follow the Seven Principles to Create a Life You Love.

http://bit.ly/Action-Journal-For-Awakening-Your-Dreams-by-Gary-Wilkin

INTRODUCTION

It all started because of a snowstorm...

I have worked nearly all my adult life, beginning a few months before I graduated from Colorado State University in 1979, until I fist-bumped my way out of Ecolab in May 2019.

My career was full of great teams and bosses, challenging projects, and fun times – even a few Friday Afternoon Clubs back in the day. And there were a few tough times: layoffs, cost-cutting, problematic clients, demanding bosses, and irritating team members.

Sound familiar?

Along the way, I enjoyed some fun times outside of work: training to play tournament table tennis, performing in a few classical guitar recitals, building a marriage, and raising a family. I even wrote a book on repurposing content for B2B marketing, which sold well under 100 copies – not my finest hour.

Early in 2018, I was getting restless in my career. I had accomplished most of my professional goals and was starting to question my relevance and contribution. At home, I kept looking for projects to keep me occupied. I began to ask myself: "What's next?"

As I looked back over my life, I had this vague sense that there were dreams I had allowed to go dormant – lost to the busyness of life. I couldn't put my finger on them. Every time I reached for them, they would tease me with a glimpse, then disappear.

I realized I needed to revive and awaken those dreams!

I wasn't alone. My colleagues and I were successful in our business and personal lives, with workweek and weekend schedules filled with fun, worthwhile activities. Yet we knew that there were things we were uniquely wired to do that remained undone.

But what were they? Where were they?

My Watershed Moment

In November 2018, I experienced a watershed moment. 'Watershed' may technically be the wrong term, though, because this pivotal moment was actually triggered by a snowstorm...

It all started on that snowy November morning as I was preparing for a brutal commute to downtown St. Paul, MN.

It had snowed five to six inches the night before, and my typical 20-minute drive was looking more like two hours. The kicker: I had an early meeting I needed to facilitate in-person – these were pre-Zoom days.

I got up early, scooped the drive (alas, no snowblower), and came back inside to get ready for work.

As I looked at myself in the mirror (not a pretty sight), I asked myself: "Do you want to do this? I mean, do you REALLY want to do this?"

A heartbeat later, I surprised myself by blurting out: "No!"

And "this" was not about the drive – it was about my career… my job… my life… the BIG "THIS"!

For the first time, I said aloud what had been skulking around in the back of my head for a while. What I was doing felt mechanical, flat, and uninspiring. I needed a change.

A Zig Ziglar quote came to mind: *"Hope is born when you understand this: you have the power to make things better or worse, and the CHOICE is yours."*

I decided to exercise my power. I chose to make my life better.

At that moment, the trajectory of my life changed. My destination was not yet clear, but I knew it was out there. I was determined to find it!

The next six months were a whirlwind of activity. I was committed to change but wasn't quite sure where to start. I read books and blogs, talked to friends, and spent time with my mentor.

I began to understand what I needed to do. Fundamentally, I started to clarify where I wanted to go next, identify what and who I needed to get there, and then take action. Simple, yet daunting.

In May 2019, I left Ecolab for the last time. My wife and I had decided to move to Phoenix to help care for my then 90-year-old father-in-law and explore other pursuits.

And so began my journey: a voyage to explore my potential and create a life I could love – one full of meaning and purpose.

Why This Book?

At the time of publication, that was a little over three years ago. I've learned a lot since then – some intentional, some trial and error. But I kept moving forward. I continued to talk to colleagues and mentors. I worked with a coach who could ask me simple questions that somehow drew out insights I didn't realize were inside me.

Experiencing the power of that coaching relationship led me to become a Licensed Ziglar Choose To Win Coach. I now combine my life experiences and the Ziglar legacy content to help professionals in the midst of their "What's next?" transition.

As I work with clients now, in this space, I realize that many – but not all – of the choices and challenges I have faced are common in the retirement transition phase of life.

I wrote Awakening Your Dreams: Seven Principles to Create a Life You Love to challenge you to think and dream about your own retirement transition phase.

Our journeys are unique. I'm here to provide a heads-up on some things you may/may not face, and perhaps draw out some insights you don't realize are in you.

I invite you to grab your journal and a friendly beverage. It's time to examine those dreams gone dormant amidst the hubbub of life and mold them into new and even more exciting dreams for the future.

Seven Principles to Create a Life You Love

I organized my thoughts into Seven Principles as I worked through my transition from a corporate professional to someone beginning to create the next chapter in my life – one where I could focus on doing those things I was uniquely wired to do that remained undone.

I hope they will spark questions and insights that will help you begin to create the life of meaning and purpose for which you yearn. They are:

1. The Principle of Choice
2. The Principle of Responsibility
3. The Principle of Purpose
4. The Principle of Goals
5. The Principle of Balance
6. The Principle of Habits and Routines
7. The Principle of Transformation

For each principle, I'll share what I learned, then ask you to pull out your journal and take action by reflecting on where you are and what you are learning. Discoveries in one principle may trigger the need to update thoughts captured for another. As you work through them, you will begin to clarify where you want to go and start to craft your path to a life full of meaning and purpose.

The Heart of the *Awakening Your Dreams* Journey

This journey of awakening your dreams is a pilgrimage of the mind and an exercise in making small, consistent choices.

The heavy lifting involves our mindset and imagination. Creating a new vision of your future will challenge your mindset and identity. Awakening your dreams and creating new ones will help you clarify what you want your life to look like and why.

With clarity, your actions will become more focused and your progress will increase. Specific targets and goals will help you identify the small choices that will become the engine of change as you travel the path to your new destination.

Standing here on the precipice of change and creating a life of meaning and purpose is exhilarating and terrifying.

Good news! The first step is simple. It all starts with a choice.

THE PRINCIPLE
OF CHOICE

HOPE IS BORN WHEN YOU UNDERSTAND THIS:
YOU HAVE THE POWER TO MAKE
THINGS BETTER OR WORSE,
AND THE CHOICE IS YOURS.

~ZIG ZIGLAR

The first principle is simple yet powerful.

We begin our journey by recognizing this simple truth: We have the power to make things better or worse in our lives.

The **Principle of Choice** says we are free to choose to exercise that power however we wish.

That's it.

We choose to make our lives better by awakening and rekindling dreams that may have gone dormant in the busyness of life and transforming them into new, vibrant dreams.

Good news! You already possess the power to choose and are free to exercise that power any way you wish.

You have everything you need to create the life you want. But the real value contained in this principle is what it gives birth to: **Hope!**

Why is hope so important? As Zig Ziglar once said, "Hope is the power that gives a person the confidence to step out and try."

The Power of Hope

Hope helps us begin and persist. Hope empowers us to adjust our path, not our destination, when we encounter obstacles.

Hope broadens our horizons. Hope allows us to awaken our dreams and transform them into something new and exciting.

Hope encourages us. Hope reminds us that this journey is worthwhile.

Hope propels us forward in our quest to create a life we love.

How One Small Choice Made the Difference

I made a choice on that snowy November morning back in 2018.

I knew that things needed to change. I made a conscious decision to make my life better, although, at that time, I wasn't sure what that looked like.

The kernel of hope created as a result of that choice fortified me with "the confidence to step out and try." I didn't have all the details figured out, but I had hope. Making that choice was the first step of my journey.

My choice led to hope, which led to action.

Time for Action:

Get out your journal and take time to ponder on paper. Remember, each of us has the power to make things better or worse in our lives – and the choice is ours.

What are some things you could do, or have done, to make your life worse?

I have found that when I jump into arguments without all the facts and begin spouting advice and directives, things very rarely work out well (that, my friend, is an understatement).

I've also started weight-lifting workouts without warming up. For days, I was reminded that I had chosen to make my life worse.

- Take a few moments – scratch out five to ten things you could do (or did do) that would make your life worse.

What are some things you could do, or have done, to make your life better?

Eventually, I learned to listen much more than I spoke. This stopped me from making things worse and helped me better understand situations. As a result, I was able to improve my life and that of those around me.

I also learned the power of gratitude. I take a few minutes every morning and evening to jot down things I am grateful for. This has made a huge difference. Not only am I more grateful, but I also have more things to be grateful for.

- Take a few moments – scratch out five to ten things you could do (or did do) that would make your life better.

What do you choose?

Do you want to do the things on the list that make things better or worse?

YOU have the power to choose – pick one.

Take time to soak in that feeling. It may be very faint, but as you come to believe that you have the power to make things better in your life, you are giving birth to the power of hope!

One Last Thing

Take the time to commemorate your choice to exercise your power to make your life better.

I still have my journal entry:

Today, I chose to make my life better by taking steps to figure out what I want to do next and what will allow me to be more of what I know I can be. I'm not sure what that is, but I'm starting today. Gary Wilkin 11/26/18

Your turn – make your choice and plant the seeds of hope!

THE PRINCIPLE OF RESPONSIBILITY

YOU ARE THE ONLY PERSON IN EXISTENCE
WHO CAN USE YOUR POTENTIAL.
IT IS AN AWESOME RESPONSIBILITY.

~ZIG ZIGLAR

You just chose to make your life better. Now we'll describe who you want to become.

The **Principle of Responsibility** says we alone possess our unique skills, talents, and potential. It's our responsibility to take the actions required to bring our uniqueness to life.

To do this, we'll look back to understand the skills, talents, and values we have already cultivated. Then, we'll look forward and imagine what we can add to create an even more exciting future.

This is how we create a vision of our future selves capable of awakening our dreams and creating new, exciting dreams.

Do we want to become a version of ourselves that is overly cautious, a bit unsure, and even uncomfortable with change?

Or do we choose to become the version of ourselves that utilizes our current gifts and newly acquired talents and expertise?

I know which one I choose. How about you?

A Musical Interlude

I've dabbled at playing classical guitar for decades, but my pursuit was never disciplined or consistent.

I realized that to play guitar beautifully, I needed to become a disciplined, organized musician – one willing to build up from the fundamentals, mastering them step-by-step. I envisioned a future version of myself playing my classical guitar and being astounded by the tone, the connection of notes, and the rhythms as they flowed from my instrument.

I enjoyed the hours of practice as I became that musician. Today, I share my music with others, allowing them to float off to their places of peace and joy as they listen.

This is just one rekindled dream that I am pursuing!

Who Do You Want to Become on Your Journey?

Remember when you were just starting out in your career or as a freshman in college. Did you have a rock-solid idea of what you wanted to do for the rest of your life? Me neither.

The Time for Action section for this principle may be the most fun you've had in a long time. I want you to have a blast daydreaming, exploring possibilities, and ignoring the word "impossible."

Take time to think back and remember dreams you have let slip below the horizon.

Next, I want you to look to the future and imagine all the inspiring things you want to be, do, and have!

Don't let yourself get intimidated by thinking there is only one thing you can ever do in the future. Hogwash! Have fun, and remember: you own your future; you drive it wherever you wish.

Time for Action:

Let's Play Some Ping-Pong

Get out your journal and set aside some time to dream and imagine and play!

Create two lists:

1. Current Skills and Talents:
    a. List your gifts, talents, skills, expertise, and values.
    b. What things have people asked you about? What comes easily to you?
    c. Ask your friends what they see as your strengths.
2. Future Skills and Talents:
    a. What new skills and expertise do you want?
    b. What makes you come alive?
    c. What amazing things can you do in the future that you never imagined possible before?
    d. Where will you add the most value?

Play a little ping-pong and create your future story:

1. Get out your two lists.

2. Bounce back and forth between your two lists and daydream. Create the most inspiring story of your future you can imagine.

   a. What gifts, talents, skills, and expertise do you possess?

   b. Who are you serving or helping in some way?

   c. What adversity or challenges have you faced? How are you using that experience and your new skills and talents to help others overcome that adversity?

   d. What does your typical day look like?

   e. Where are you? Who are you with?

   f. How do you feel when you wake up? Excited? Joyful?

   g. How do you feel as you look back on your day? Grateful? Fulfilled?

   h. Create as much detail as you can!

   i. Have fun as you daydream on paper!

Congratulations! You've just painted a picture of the future you want to create!

As you make this story come to life, how you see yourself, your behavior, and your mission will change.

What is your purpose behind this dream? Let's find out!

THE PRINCIPLE
OF PURPOSE

THE HEART OF HUMAN EXCELLENCE OFTEN BEGINS
TO BEAT WHEN YOU DISCOVER A PURSUIT THAT
ABSORBS YOU, FREES YOU, CHALLENGES YOU, OR
GIVES YOU A SENSE OF MEANING, JOY, OR PASSION.

~ TERRY ORLICK, PhD

Knowing your purpose helps you "discover a pursuit that absorbs you," changing every aspect of your life.

The **Principle of Purpose** says that behind our future dream lies a purpose. Understanding why we are pursuing it and the value it brings motivates us to keep going even as obstacles emerge and enthusiasm wanes.

You may be wondering how to uncover the purpose behind your dream for the future.

Let me share a story about how I approached it.

How I Came to Write This Book

I have prided myself on being able to take complex ideas and communicate them simply. I used this "superpower" to help my colleagues understand complex issues and make better decisions. On that snowy November morning, I realized that figuring out what was next was not a simple problem. It was time to use my "superpower" again.

As I read books, talked to coaches, and chatted with friends, I distilled the core issues that drive a successful transformation.

To transform, you need to do three things: choose to change, dream a big dream, and take action.

I shared this simple formula with a few friends. Their eyes lit up, their shoulders straightened, and they smiled, saying, "I can do this!"

I continued to work to validate my assumptions. I made my choice and began to dream my big dream. I saw myself as a speaker and author sharing the *Awakening Your Dreams* model. I could hear the applause and feel the satisfaction of helping people address their own challenges with crafting a life of meaning and purpose.

As I envisioned my future, I pulled out my journal and captured all the details I could imagine.

Next, I asked: Why do I want to do this?

I want to empower my fellow business professionals to choose to create a compelling vision of their future.

How will this help my audience?

They will experience the power of choice as they create a compelling future and take action to bring it to life.

I realized *Awakening Your Dreams* could be summarized as choosing to change, dreaming a big dream, and taking action.

That's when I knew I needed to write this book.

I want to share with you that if you choose to change, dream a big dream, and take action, you can build a compelling vision of your future and bring it to life.

Remember, our journeys are unique. What fascinates me may not interest you at all. I want you to understand the underlying process and how you can use it to create your own fabulous future.

How to uncover the purpose behind your dream for the future.

Our purpose becomes the filter for everything we do from this point forward. Every choice, every decision we make, is evaluated based on how well it supports our purpose.

Our purpose answers the question: "Why am I doing this?"

Understanding our purpose gives us power, resilience, and grit as we become the kind of person who can live out our life filled with meaning and purpose.

Time for Action:

OK, pull out your journal and re-read your dream story several times.

See it in your mind. Hear the voices around you, smell the foods cooking in the kitchen or the fresh mountain air. See yourself there – living your life of meaning and purpose.

With that vision clear in your mind, think on paper as you ask yourself some questions to clarify why you want it to become your new reality:

- Why do I want this vision of my future? What is my motivation?
- What about it is the most appealing?
- What will it accomplish? Who will it help?

- What problems am I solving?
- Where am I adding the most value?
- How will accomplishing it make me feel?
- How will it add value to my life and those around me?

And a few more…

- Is this my vision or what someone else thinks I should want?
- Is it primarily about what I can get, or does it involve what I can give?

If your purpose is primarily self-centered, I urge you to consider how this dream can be used to serve and help others. Involving others as part of the purpose behind your dream adds power and motivation as you seek to make that dream come to life.

As you ponder and answer these questions, you may need to refine the vision of your future. That's fine – it's normal. Go ahead, tweak it, review the prompts, and update your journal.

Quick Reflection

As you wrap up this section, I want you to stop and look back to the day before you picked up this book.

Now, think about where you are today.

You've chosen to begin a journey to make things better in your life. You've described this life in detail and taken the time to understand how pursuing and living that life helps you and others.

You have described *"a pursuit that absorbs you, frees you, challenges you, or gives you a sense of meaning, joy, or passion."*

That is no small accomplishment. Congratulations!

Now, let's begin to bring that vision to life.

THE PRINCIPLE
OF GOALS

WHAT YOU GET BY ACHIEVING YOUR GOALS
IS NOT AS IMPORTANT AS WHAT YOU BECOME
BY ACHIEVING YOUR GOALS.

~ZIG ZIGLAR

Your journal now contains an inspiring story that describes a life that *"gives you a sense of meaning, joy, or passion,"* and why you want it!

Let's bring it to life!

The **Principle of Goals** says that the primary focus of goals is to help you become the kind of person capable of living out your life of purpose.

All of us have had our fill of goal-setting books and seminars. Some helped me. Others not so much. How about you? Recently, I had a breakthrough in this area as I intentionally focused on the "why" of goal setting versus the mechanics. This chapter is a result of that breakthrough.

A good friend of mine, Jackie Listen, shared a great story about how setting one goal improved his health and self-confidence. His story makes me smile every time I hear him tell it.

The First Step Is the Hardest

I'd been working on my health for eight years – eating better, going to the gym, running up to three miles a few times a week.

In my December 2010 goal-setting session with two close friends, I announced:

"Gentlemen, I'm 49! I'm committing to run the half marathon in OKC – all 13.1 miles!"

"Are you serious?"

"Yes! And you two are going to hold me accountable!"

"OK, we'll run the 5K at the same race!"

Walking out of that meeting, it hit me: "How am I going to do this?!?" So, I googled "half marathon rookie" and found a plan I could do!

I entered the Memorial Half Marathon in OKC set for May 2011 – less than six months away! I set a goal to run the race in under two hours!

There were days when I didn't "feel" like running, but I had made a commitment to my friends, and I knew that pursuing my goal required consistency and grit.

I was reminded every morning: the first step is always the hardest!

Fast-forward to May 1, 2011. The starter gun sounds, and I take off with the crowd. 13.1 miles later, my race timer read 1:51:39!

I did it!

Not only had I finished my first half marathon, but I beat my target time by almost nine minutes!

I sat down on the sidewalk and thought: "Wow! If I could set my mind to accomplish this goal, imagine what else I can set my mind to achieve!"

How did Jackie do this? He committed to a goal, understood the benefits, gathered resources, recruited friends to support him, and followed his plan.

Jackie experienced the power of setting and achieving goals: he had become a healthier and more confident version of himself!

Essential Elements of a Good Goal-Setting Approach

In his book, *Choose to Win*, Tom Ziglar shares an interesting conversation with Bob Tiede *(https:// leadingwithquestions.com/)*. Bob shared "only 20% of people are excited about setting and working on goals, while the other 80% are primarily motivated by solving problems." Feel free to frame this principle as achieving goals or solving problems, whichever you prefer.

The essential elements of a good goal-setting/ problem-solving approach will:

- help you choose the right goal.
- create hope and belief that pursuing the goal is worthwhile.
- encourage the relentless pursuit of the goal.

Choosing the Right Goal

Choosing the right goal is the most critical element of any goal-setting system. Why? All the time and effort pursuing the wrong goal is lost time. I don't want to waste my time, do you?

The right goal:

- is your goal, not what someone else thinks you should be or do.
- is about becoming who **you** need to be to live your life of meaning and purpose.
- is consistent with your values and principles and does not force you to compromise your morals.
- doesn't conflict with your other goals. e.g. a goal that requires a lot of time away from home (i.e. golfing) conflicts with a goal of spending more time with family.

The right goal(s) will help you become the kind of person capable of living the life you described in your journal.

Belief That This Is a Worthwhile Goal

You'll work harder to achieve a goal you believe is worthwhile versus one you don't.

A great goal-setting system helps you filter out those "good but not great goals" before you spend much time planning them out. This filter is applied to your "right goals" list.

Right goals transform your life. Worthwhile goals enable you to transform yourself and impact others as well. A broader span of impact will enhance your commitment and enthusiasm as you pursue that goal.

Encouraging Daily Action

Setting a goal is not achieving a goal. It's a great start, but don't pat yourself on the back just yet.

Achieving a goal requires action.

The best goal-setting systems help you build momentum by encouraging consistent, directed action to achieve your goal.

Consistent action starts in the mind as you review and recite your goals daily. This creates a mindset focused on the value of the goal, the benefits of achieving the goal, and becoming the person you need to be to live your life of meaning and purpose.

This focused mindset then produces the actions required to achieve the goal. As Jackie related, he didn't always feel like running, but he took that hard first step because he knew that was how he would achieve his half marathon goal.

Daily action is reinforced by creating and tracking simple habits and routines.

Working with a great accountability partner radically increases your success rate! John Lee Dumas, of Entrepreneur On Fire fame, shares: "I cannot count the number of accomplishments I've had or the number of goals I've reached as a specific result of my accountability partner being there for me."

A great goal-setting system focuses you on the right goals, for the right reasons, so that you become the kind of person who can live out your life of meaning and purpose.

It's about inner transformation!

Time for Action:

Grab your journal and review the story you created and revised in the Principles of Responsibility and Purpose Time for Action exercises.

As you reread your story, look for skills, knowledge, or relationships you need to develop or enhance to become the person capable of living out that story.

Most of my clients have worked through multiple goal-setting systems during their careers. I have found that the Ziglar Goal Setting System is one of the most effective, yet simple approaches to crafting and achieving goals.

The key steps are:

- *Create a list of the right goals*
- *Ensure they are worthwhile goals*
- *Create detailed goal statements*
- *Analyze and prioritize goals*
- *Plan daily execution, tracking, and review*
- *Get an accountability partner*
- *Celebrate completions, update the active list*

If you have a preferred goal-setting system, feel free to stick with it. If you are interested in reviewing or using the Ziglar Goal Setting System, you can download a free copy at:

https://myretirementmission.com/downloads/

I have also created a short video explaining the key points of using the Ziglar system. You can check it out at:

https://myretirementmission.com/videos/

Whatever system you use, now is the time to create your initial set of goals that will enable you to live the life you painted in your future story. This can take some time, but the return on your effort is well worth it!

What's Next?

You are making tremendous progress in awakening your dreams as you transform your life into one of meaning and purpose!

Next, let's see what balanced success looks like as you continue the journey forward.

THE PRINCIPLE
OF BALANCE

Focusing on one or two areas of your life at the expense of the others – something we have all done at one time or another – is a recipe for disaster.

The focus of the **Principle of Balance** is to take an honest look at your life and ensure you are approaching the pursuit of your dreams in a balanced way.

Several tools will allow you to examine the quality of different aspects (spokes) of your life. I've seen tools that use as few as four areas and as many as ten or more.

I prefer the seven-spoke model used in the Choose To Win Coaching Program – it's simple yet comprehensive. The seven spokes are:

Mental: What you choose to think about determines
            everything about how you live.

Spiritual:	Spiritual principles and values you live by either unleash or limit your potential.
Physical:	Providing consistent and persistent fuel to your body helps you maintain a healthy lifestyle.
Family:	Choose to be a positive influence by being a good example.
Financial:	Making wise financial decisions inspires hope and builds your dreams.
Personal:	Use your time and energy wisely.
Career:	Choose true performance over uninspired activity.

Again, if you have found a life balance/wheel of life tool you like, feel free to use it. If you would like to look at the Ziglar Wheel of Life assessment, you can download your free copy here: *https://myretirementmission.com/downloads/*

I recommend you take time to walk through this or your preferred assessment periodically. Do it today as part of your *Awakening Your Dreams* journey. It will help guide you as you review your goals and prepare to build habits and routines in the areas needing the most attention.

Set a calendar appointment to take it again three months from now and compare the results. I know I was surprised by the changes at my three-month mark.

Lessons Learned

I learned the value of this principle the old-fashioned way – I messed up.

- *For a decade and a half, I was on the road extensively, making great strides in my career while abdicating the responsibility of raising my family to my wife. Career over Family – not good.*
- *While pursuing advanced degrees in Computer Science, I neglected my health and gained over 40 pounds. Personal over Health – not good either.*
- *I often worked over the weekend and neglected to attend church. Career over Spiritual – not a winning strategy.*

The key lesson here is to compare the balance you currently have in your life with the focus of the goals you have identified. Do you have goals that will help you pay special attention to those areas needing growth, but not at the expense of ignoring other aspects of your life?

Time for Action:

This exercise provides another filter for the goals you have defined in the **Principle of Goals**.

Grab your journal.

Download and print your copy of the Wheel of Life Assessment, or your preferred tool.

- Take the assessment and map out where you are on each spoke.
- Review your master goal list and ensure you have at least one goal focusing on each area of your life.

Are you addressing all the areas of your life? Are your initial goals focusing on the areas that need the most work?

Goals provide the overall direction for our lives. It's important to ensure we are pursuing a balanced life with a set of well-rounded goals.

Habits and routines will be what we execute daily to achieve our goals.

Let's see how easy it is to create new habits and routines.

THE PRINCIPLE OF
HABITS AND ROUTINES

A HABIT IS SIMPLY A GOOD SMALL CHOICE
DONE OVER AND OVER AGAIN.

~TOM ZIGLAR

By now, you have logged a lot of journal time. The vision of your ideal future is becoming clearer. You've assessed the needs in different areas of your life and have built a balanced list of goals to bring your vision to life. Now, let's turn it into a daily pursuit!

The **Principle of Habits and Routines** says that taking small, consistent action is how we achieve our goals and create a life full of meaning and purpose.

We often hear that "change is hard." Good news! Properly formed habits and routines take the "hard" out of change.

Habits are simply good choices we make over and over again.

Routines are groups of habits we combine to help perform more complex tasks.

How do we create habits that stick?

BJ Fogg, PhD, author of *Tiny Habits – The Small Changes That Change Everything,* has created a unique approach to creating new habits. This website provides an overview by Dr. Fogg: https://tinyhabits.com/design/.

He says that when you create a new habit, it needs to be so small (tiny) that even on your worst day, you can do it with little or no resistance.

He uses a simple "A-B-C" recipe:

1. **Anchor Moment:** This is something you already do regularly that will remind you to do your new Tiny Behavior.
2. **Tiny Behavior:** This is typically a miniature version of the habit you want to create. BJ Fogg uses the example of flossing just one tooth as the perfect size for a Tiny Behavior. The key is that you perform this behavior immediately after the Anchor Moment.
3. **Celebration:** Immediately after completing the behavior, pump your fist or smile and say, "I did it!" Celebrate the fact you did it! These little acknowledgements help cement the Tiny Behavior as something that makes your brain feel good when you do it.

How do habits help us Awaken Our Dreams?

As you live out your ideal future, you will need to do things differently than you do now. The goals and plans of action define the milestones to help you become the kind of person who can live out that life of meaning and purpose.

Habits and routines are how you will change your behavior and achieve those goals. If you try to brute force your way into change, you will be disappointed. Think about all the New Year's Resolutions you've kept. Right, I can't think of any either.

Habits allow us to start small (tiny) and grow them. BJ's "floss one tooth" habit seems silly, doesn't it? But it helped me begin to floss my teeth regularly in the evening. Mornings were fine, but I needed a simple A-B-C recipe to help me consistently floss in the evening.

The power of tiny habits is that they train your brain to show up and start.

Starting is the hardest part of any change. Taking tiny steps makes it easier to begin a new behavior. You can then slowly expand to the point where you are flossing all your teeth regularly or accomplishing whatever you are trying to do.

As you look at your action plans, identify what things you will need to do regularly – these are candidates for tiny habits.

As you create new tiny habits, you can stack them together to make routines.

1. Create your first habit from an anchor moment already in place.
2. Use the completion of that tiny habit as the anchor moment for the next habit.
3. Then use that tiny habit to anchor another, and so on.

Creating My Reading Habit

After I left corporate, I struggled with reading consistently. I had been reading every day while on the bus to and from work, but obviously, those days were gone (yaay!).

I tried to read consistently, but I couldn't get in the groove. So, I turned to BJ Fogg's Tiny Habit approach and followed his Anchor-Behavior-Celebration method to create a tiny habit recipe:

After I finish my morning cup of coffee, I will read one page. As I flip the page (or swipe it), I will smile, and say to myself, "'Good job!"

That's it!

As I committed to doing this daily, reading one page became a natural part of my morning. Eventually, I read a few more pages each day – but my commitment was to read just one page. I just needed a way to start reading each day. My total reading expanded from there.

Let's see what you can do.

Time for Action:

Identify some habits that will help you achieve your goals.

- Review your story to remind you of what you want to be, do, and have in the future.
- Pull out your current goals sheets and review your plan of action to reach the goal.
- What action(s) will you need to do that you are not currently doing?
- Apply the A-B-C method to create a tiny version of this action.

- Write out your Tiny Habit Recipe and start!
- Extra credit: build a routine combining multiple tiny habits.

What's Ahead?

The final principle, the **Principle of Transformation**, will pull everything together and show the master view of *Awakening Your Dreams*!

THE PRINCIPLE OF TRANSFORMATION

> YOU ARE WHO YOU ARE AND WHAT YOU ARE
> BECAUSE OF WHAT HAS GONE INTO YOUR MIND.
> YOU CAN CHANGE WHO YOU ARE AND WHAT YOU
> ARE BY CHANGING WHAT GOES INTO YOUR MIND.
>
> ~ZIG ZIGLAR

What does it mean to transform?

Early in my journey, I told my friends that transformation required just three things: choose to change, dream big, and take action. As I've grown these past few years, I have added depth and nuance to that formula.

The first six Principles presented the foundational tactics and actions of the transformation journey. This Principle reflects the strategic view of transformation. I hope it helps you understand the core elements in your pursuit to transform – to become someone new.

The Principle of Transformation rests on the relationships among desire, hope, and grit:

Desire:	A clear (and possibly evolving) view of what you truly want.
Hope:	The belief that fulfilling your desires will give your life meaning and purpose.
Grit:	Relentless action to identify and develop the skills, relationships, attitudes, and beliefs that will help you become the person capable of achieving your desires.

We began this journey by making the choice to make our lives better. We articulated our *desire* as we described in detail how we wanted to display our unique skills, talents, and potential in the future.

We then developed *hope* as we clarified the purpose – the why – behind our desired future: a future designed to create a life of meaning and purpose.

Finally, we began to set up the structure for the relentless action (*grit*) required to bring this vision to pass by creating balanced goals and daily habits and routines to ensure growth.

The most critical aspect of transformation remains the mindset. What we allow into our minds determines who we are. When we change what we allow into our minds, we change.

I Hated the Mirror

I had ballooned up to over 240 pounds on a frame designed for a bit under 200. My blood work was deteriorating, I felt like crap, and I knew I needed to change... now!

I consulted my doctor and a nutritionist to develop an overall plan of action and target timeline.

Before we started creating new meal plans and exercise routines, my wife and I spent time listing all the benefits of losing weight. We visualized our life as we ate healthy food and exercised for fun and enjoyment. We saw ourselves going to the store to buy new clothes, getting up refreshed every morning, and participating in fun social activities. Then we committed to working our butts off (pun intended) to make the change.

When things got tough, we pulled out our list and reminded ourselves why we were doing this.

After six months of making countless small, good choices (and a few poor ones), I stepped on the scales at the doctor's office – you know, the ones that add *ten* pounds automatically!

Victory! It read 199.4 pounds!

In partnership with my wife, I had changed! I was a lighter person. I saw food and exercise differently. I had gained confidence by making decisions and taking action long after the excitement was over. I had experienced the power of a caring accountability partner. I had transformed.

Transformation and Awakening Your Dreams

Zig Ziglar reminds us that we are who we are and what we are because of what has gone into our minds. We're here today because of the choices we have made.

He also tells us that you can change who you are and what you are by changing what goes into your mind. Inner transformation is a choice.

This is not a one-and-done journey. As you travel down your path, you will see even further. You will be inspired to make even more changes and develop even larger visions of your future.

Time for Action:

You now have the roadmap. "The Seven Principles to Create A Life You Love" are now available to you!

I encourage you to use them, tweak them, and make them yours. I also urge you to share with those you love. Let your transformation be the spark for change in those around you.

Leave a legacy of change, one of extraordinary futures only you can bring to life.

One day, you will look back and realize how far you've come. As you turn around again, you'll see all the new dreams stretching out before you. Take a moment to smile.

Remember, this all started with a choice.

THE JOURNEY AHEAD

WHO CARES WHO YOU'VE BEEN.
WHO DO YOU WANT TO BE?

~ BENJAMIN HARDY

What have you learned about yourself as you have taken action and written in your journal?

Do you see a future brimming with hope as you live a life full of meaning and purpose?

Earlier, I noted that standing here on the precipice of change and creating a life of meaning and purpose is both exhilarating and terrifying.

You are on that precipice. You have a choice. Push forward and create a life of meaning and purpose. Take risks and pursue new ideas relentlessly. Or, you can say, "No thanks, I'm good."

That was the real question I asked myself in the mirror that snowy November morning.

Did I want to continue living a mechanical, flat, and uninspiring life? Or did I want to pursue things I was uniquely wired to do that remained undone?

This is the call of inner transformation.

As you choose and commit to what you want to be, do, and have in the future, you will develop the hope and belief that that future is one of meaning and purpose. You will stop at nothing to get there!

I believe in you and your power to create a lasting legacy befitting your life. I close with the quote that started us on the path:

> HOPE IS BORN WHEN YOU UNDERSTAND THIS:
> YOU HAVE THE POWER TO MAKE
> THINGS BETTER OR WORSE,
> AND THE CHOICE IS YOURS.
>
> ~ZIG ZIGLAR

Thank you for taking your time to read this book and work through the Seven Principles to Create a Life You Love.

I hope you will continue to apply these Principles as you move forward in your quest to create a future full of hope, meaning, and purpose.

As I have grown these past few years, I've learned the importance of having partners to encourage and challenge me. They reminded me to look back to appreciate my progress and to look forward to refocus on my goals. They helped me remember why I was on this journey.

That's where I can help you. As a partner in your journey, I can come alongside you and provide a structure of support and encouragement as you design and create a life you love. Together, we will work through the choices and actions needed to help you bring it to fruition.

I invite you to schedule a friendly 20-minute conversation to understand where you want to go and if I can help you get there. Also, we will identify at least one actionable step you can take immediately to move you in the direction of your dreams.

To schedule this complimentary 20-minute call, go to:

https://myretirementmission.com/

Feel free to connect or follow me on LinkedIn, where I share my thoughts and insights into the process of transformation:

https://www.linkedin.com/in/garywilkin/

I believe in you and the power of choice to change your life forever.

FREE RESOURCE:

Gain clarity and take action as you create a life you love.